Impossible Object

Also by Lisa Sewell:

The Way Out
Name Withheld

Impossible Object

poems by

Lisa Sewell

WINNER OF THE 2014 TENTH GATE PRIZE

THE WORD WORKS
WASHINGTON, D.C.

First Edition, First Printing
Impossible Object

The Word Works
PO Box 42164
Washington, D.C. 20015
WordWorksBooks.org

LCCN: 2015934561
ISBN: 978-0-915380-96-1

Cover design: Susan Pearce Design
Author photograph: Anne Saint Peter
Cover art: Endi Poskovic

ACKNOWLEDGMENTS

Grateful acknowledgment is made to the editors of the following publications and web-based journals in which some of these poems, or earlier versions of them, first appeared:

The Academy of American Poets Poem-a-Day, *American Letters & Commentary*, *Colorado Review*, *Crab Orchard Review*, *Denver Quarterly*, *Drunken Boat*, *Fox Chase Review*, *Harvard Review*, *The Journal*, *Laurel Review*, *Mead*, *Prairie Schooner*, *Salamander*, *Truck*, and *Tampa Review*. "The House of Bernarda Alba" appeared in *Big Bridge*, vol. 2. "The Anatomy of Melancholy" also appears in *The New American Poetry of Engagement* (McFarland, 2012).

I also wish to thank Ron Mohring at Seven Kitchens Press for publishing the chapbook *Long Corridor*, in which some of these poems also appeared, and G.C. Waldrep, who chose it for the 2008 Keystone Chapbook Prize.

I am grateful to my colleagues at Villanova for their support and to the university for a sabbatical leave that supported the completion of this manuscript. Many thanks as well to Eric Doyle and Christine Kelley for their help. The Jentel Artist Residency and the Virginia Center for the Creative Arts also provided much needed time and space.

Thanks to Nathalie Anderson, Ellen Geist, Eamon Grennan, Ann Keniston, Elaine Terranova, Claudia Rankine, and Suzanne Wise for your wisdom, patience, and generosity. Thanks as well to Endi Poskovic and to the wonderful, supportive people at The Word Works, especially Nancy White and Leslie McGrath. And to John for everything.

CONTENTS

The Poetics of Space

In memory of
George Joseph Sewell, 1908-2011
Dorothy Sewell Blake, 1922-2014

It is what you read when you don't have to that determines what you will be when you can't help it.

—Oscar Wilde

Who are we, who is each one of us, if not a combinatoria of experiences, information, books we have read, things imagined?

—Italo Calvino

The lives of which I read seemed more real than my own, but I still seemed more real than the persons who had led them.

—Lyn Hejinian

Long Corridor

O summon me,
first to the porter's compartment
to question in private my whereabouts
and wardrobe, sleeping habits and origins,

then with all the other passengers on the Orient Express—
the elder statesman, *the small dark man*
with a womanish voice—
to the velvet curtained rail car scene of crimes.

And in the voice of reason, tone that holds its own
but hoards its shocking revelations
until the very end, tell what we have done.

Be diminutive and mild or darkly French
with waxed mustaches but choose an English
and explanation each of us can believe

and as pieces fall, as clouds disperse, expose
the mottled clear blue entrails underneath.

Show me the knife, my fingerprints
on the cabinet door, *the sound of a tap running,*
a splashing noise, the burned village
nightly body count and full terrain
of my part and my complicity

now that I am no longer young, and no longer free
to point a knowing finger, or vanish
with the flamingo kimono
down the long corridor of history.

Remembrance of Things Past

To the Lighthouse

In the narrow room, just barely just enough
for dresser, student bed, with corridor voices
leaking through the plasterboard dorm walls,
I lay on my back, book anchored,
elbows fixed and *read and turned the page,*
swinging herself from one line to another
and everything open suddenly opened:
for *beneath the color there was the shape—*
everything shifting, here or elsewhere
or a day before, or a month before that.

On the winter sand of southern California,
edgy nervous at the edge and fault line
of seventeen, with the Pacific feeling
no longer washing over me, where winter waves
bathe and blur the here and there, the wet and now
steady and moving echoes that were speaking quietly
with bravado and not to me in busy hallways
and from other rooms, like sentences that made
and saw and didn't separate: Mr. Tansley
and Mr. Ramsay and Mr. Bankes all jammed
behind and to the side and after the reappearing *he.*

And for the first time I thought, I too
was what words took and continued making
and in a slow dawning on the dorm bed
or on the sliding winter sand beneath my back
there was scarcely anything left of body or mind
by which one could say, "This is he" or "This is she,"
as though the war was on and I was in a waiting
room trying to stop myself from falling—
lying back against the sand to keep the ocean
seeming mirror still and mirror flat.

And suddenly I knew there wasn't anyone
to tell me where the ocean stopped and I began
or if the long anticipated journey, and what
would happen next. *Like a wave, which bore*
one up and threw one down with it,
there with a dash on the beach, I wondered
who would choose and how to weather
what beached my body on the sand or perched
lightly in the narrow moving floating room.

Miles away and close enough to hear them singing,
sighing fully in their bodies beneath the oceanic
mirror skin, the swimmers and floaters, gastropods
and sponges, jellyfish, diatoms and elephant seals,
who must rise to breathe with mammal lungs were moving
deliberately without pause and without deliberation
and I was more exactly not myself than anyone I
had ever met reflected in the mirrored surface
of the ocean's depth, now and in these paragraphs
like rooms that I had never seen but always lived in.

Grief Universe

The first suggestion comes in sleep, cold weeks
before the cold machinery begins
to lay its somber packages at your door:
the canny premonition, not within
the dazzling matter of the dream itself—
those unbending legs of violence
that cannot be named or felt—but in the starting
up and into the inconsolable that has
no source, no street signs, no aftertaste or origin.

Months later in the movie theater on 59th
with the known and reliable in shambles,
a story nothing like yours rapidly unfolding
across the screen, the low unmentionable
chord returns, a bell that climbs from murky
depths, a blue widening of rings.

Suddenly you realize, you are
the sudden I, the realize—
the waking dream and nightmare too,

for every time you stand at a crossroads,
you have two universes before you
and if you emigrate to a life
of strangers, *it's entirely a personal matter*—

The abiding violent anti-hunger, the empty
grief *universe in front of you*, becomes inhabitation
final and complete, though no longer in the ways,
deep in the suburbs of Los Angeles
we had always talked about and longed for.

The Anatomy of Melancholy

Apt to loathe, dislike, disdain, and weary
when the heart-strings do burn and beat,
and the heart itself faints like fits of the mother,

he said he wanted everything to end,
not to be in my compact car
discussing wishes and requiring analysis,

to be inert and without meaning,
as uninterpreted as *those who cannot tell*
to express themselves in words or how it holds them.

*

I do things slowly.
The future seems endless.
I am bothered by things that do not affect me.

*

Now the chest, now belly and sides,
then heart and head aches,
now heat, then wind, now this, now that—

When the Sunday bomber blew
at a funeral in Tikrit and we argued
again, and he spent another night

hard sleeping on his cluttered office floor
to keep the indignation clean and glowing,
at least fifteen were killed and seventeen wounded.

*

The researchers repeated the experiment three times,
zeroing in on the amygdala, thimble-sized trigger point

for fear and craving and wild euphoric highs
that sits two inches behind the bridge of the nose.

He is weary of all and yet will not, cannot tell
how, where, or what offends him.

The colonel said no coalition soldier
was responsible for the murder of that family,
the rape and murder of that little girl.

*

I am all appetite.
I have crying spells.
It is hard to concentrate on reading.

*

And though very modest of themselves,
sober, religious, virtuous and well given,
they cannot make resistance and are violently
carried away with this inward torrent of humors.

Refugees fleeing bombardment
talked of chemical attacks and people melting,
pieces of bombs exploding in fires
that burn the skin even when water is applied.

So when he lay face down on the bed
in broad daylight, all the curtains drawn,
and said, "I wish I was dead,"
why did I correct his grammar?

It may be the most detailed snapshot
ever taken, mapping melancholy
on the gray matter of the brain

and exactly what goes wrong
in a mind overwhelmed
by the downward spiral of despair.

*

Everything I do is an effort.
My sleep is restless.
I'm not as good as other people.
I have trouble keeping my mind.

Fastened onto one thing without an ague,
better marry than burn saith the apostles
but they are otherwise persuaded.

He was going to get a memorial tattoo
of all the guys who were killed
but there was no more room on his arm
below the elbow.

In the parking lot, we parted,
despondent and prone to weeping,
so far gone, so stupefied with distraction,
we thought ourselves charmed
or bewitched.

Bad Faith

Was the bitter one. Was the apple
of unkind, like Margery Kempe
who *slandered her husband,*
her friends, her own self.

Was the frown and unforgiving face
that hovers spite-filled, known and unfamiliar
in the plate glass window light.

Was the bad-faith sorry and the yes
please, and could not put a name
or too fine a point on it, much less
defend an outlook or a point of view

for as the spirits tempted her to say
and do, so she said and so she did.

Sharp enough for stitchery, words too
could pierce the skin's indifference,
moving in and out like quick machinery,
a steady rows of flames.

And from this seat on the long hill of time,
I can read the devilish postpartum
blues that bite through her own skin
and drive her toward the careful negotiation:

forsooth, I had liefer see my husband slain
than we should turn again to our uncleanness—

She had a pilgrimage, a choice to make
just as I have made and unmade mine:

the umber wool sweater still murmurs from
the knitting bag, half the front, most
of the back, no collar, and one full arm.

Middlemarch

not afterwards, which hadn't arrived

not afterwards, but during the still remarkably lively and alert, still rising, urged forward by daylight, the phone's ring, the birthdays arriving, Julys and Novembers of one-hundred-and-one, one-hundred-and-three, *like hearing the grass grow and the squirrel's heart beat*

in the cadence and moans that shake their heads: not shooting or dull, not sharp, not throbbing, not between or behind the eyes where words fail and there's not a God-damned thing anyone can do about it anyway

when no one could express or understand, or stand, no doctor or nurse, for no any or one can know how a body and this skin, this field of blotch and darken can't bear even the mild palliative care or even whisper for *we should die of that roar*

like the fluttering heartbeat swollen ankle breathlessness excoriating unnamable pain that cannot be put into words or made to climb the sinews and clarities of a Victorian sentence

with the lists of names and places on scraps and sheets piled beside the phone, the TV, on the nightstand: Pancho Villa, radiation, Joanne Woodward, huckleberry, Houston Street, Ambien, mockingbird, gooseberry, Danny Kaye, Fidel Castro, Dirty Harry, Katz's Deli and mockingbird, mockingbird, mockingbird

long before the thinking through and finding of sentences, or deciding exactly how to put it on the page and where to pause and what to catalog and when to let the white space widen, as *if we had a keen vision and feeling of all ordinary human life*

and from the kitchen hearing how the well guarded borders
of individuals fail in the abscess that can be soothed but never
healed, in the Byzantine and shallow breathing, *which lies on
the other side of silence*

afterwards only seemed to lurk fox-like along the emptying
dirt roads and hairpin mountain turns of thought and
thinking

from this side, not to pine or rail, demand the what and how
and fulfillment of prescriptions, the when and precisely where
the pain did settle in and how to fix it

when there is never a where or right place to break the line
and yet there and there again the line must be broken.

Diary of a Young Girl

Sister and first love
to every girl's first loss

and first sadness, she taught
the consolations and shock

of newsreeled bodies, the martyred
face filling the screen

of our imaginings and all the long women
nodding yes at the pressing—

and the boots on the ground
of catalog and secret keeping,

granting permission to track and bemoan
mother with her shortcomings,

her careless sarcasm and hard-heartedness—
to hide indecipherable longings with code.

But the mind is a fabulator: those mornings
and long nights dyed the blue gray of hiding

were never mine. The darkling eyes
and heart's wish, *the wonderful glow*

that made up for all the rest,
could not stave off the swaths of never days,

the girlish body measured and stamped,
whittled down and translated to fever and can't.

A body of water never breaks down
when starved, when beaten.

In photosynthesis the Calvin cycle
or dark reactions reduce carbon dioxide

to sugar, but you cannot turn
the fretful child into a tranquil adult

or prevent the feeding frenzy in the fish tank.
Under stars, breathing air

with embarrassment and rue,
the others are ones remembering her too.

In my grandmother's English they still dream
of swimming in bodies while the smoke blew.

Four Years of Days

For seven years, on four of seven days I walked
or biked or rode the subway to her real wood paneling
and sat at first, then lay so that my eyes were free
to ride the airy currents of that room, so like *the sharp point*
into which all light converged, or an afternoon without need
or obligation, or reading Henry James on the overnight train
across the golden bowl of the Indian subcontinent.

When my father's legs came into view, I said
I dreamed an endless stream of cars in gridlock,
the words very much as if they were blue daylight
and jam she said, and I said Sunday mornings bittersweet
or buckwheat pancakes weekend mornings—
knowing I had failed again, to unearth the phrase or sentence
that would disclose the gears and workings of the real.

We played across a hidden net, my lobs and volleys
never met, or I was on the witness stand
pleading innocent to the prosecuting voice that knew
the withheld crimes, the guilt, all the hard evidence
and waited patiently, *even if the thing should come to pieces*,
for the memory or dream to speak
from deep within the locked safe of reminiscence.

For four years on four of seven days she put me
through my paces or so it seemed until the early
Cambridge snowbound morning I finally understood:
the bowl, *it doesn't break like vile glass, it splits*
and for all those months of mornings there was no one
to rally against, only the one who was supposed
to know, keeping pace and hurrying, beside me.

King Lear

For the father who wakes
and wakes himself, eyes full of himself

and for the one who, when the sun descends,
slips into the stormy,

smite flat the rotundity o' the world.

Done in with conspiracy and murder
in his sleep (his eye-tooth finally unfixed
and tucked into a cheek for safekeeping),

he dreams of a three-armed garment,
unable to wonder or comprehend
how he has come to this blurred ridge and broken—

I try to fix in my mind his shining eyes,
the terrors he shut his lips against

and his early morning utterly lucid accusation:
"I never would have believed," he said to me,
"that you would be among them."

The Corrections

Now that someone isn't speaking to me
in places we are meant to share,

though beside myself,
I am no longer in the vicinity.

My questions shudder toward an ear
that is no corridor

but a series of corrections,
a door become implacable wall,

while outside, the wind has blown the sun out
and it is getting very cold.

The open room of respond and comprehend
unopens and I have access only to

what shutters the relentless,
clothed in outrage and reproach.

How strange to say again and again
and with each repeat unravel further into naught

with everyone else still there or here
and hearing the abrupt disappear

that no one notes or notices,
that paints my skin invisible

and cloaks me in avoid,
now that someone isn't speaking to me.

Beyond the Pleasure Principle

Obliged to repeat what is repressed
as a current experience, instead of
recollecting it as a fragment of the past,
to save us, to save myself,

unpour the water from the floor,
return the piss, the seed,
unbreak the phosphorescent tubes,
the tibia and fingerbones,
the fingernails and skin,
the eardrums and the will—

detach the wires, erase the words,
unhood, unbag, unstack
the human pyramid of harms.

Return them to their real names,
return the clothing and shoes,
the water and food, the mattresses
and one hundred fifty-one nights of sleep.

Reprivate and reprieve, unmake
the bad night and bad day to follow.
Uncoil the concertina wire,
the black site and chemical light
through the dream life that takes the patient back
to the situation of his disaster
from which he awakens in renewed terror.

Take us back along the convoluted
daisy-chain of command, away
from a few bad apples
letting off steam, the kids being kids,

back to the blue light
of the screen that glows
in my living room and animates my office,
where what has changed
is only what we know and insist,

as one of the talking heads explains:
in Islam there is a need to wash the shame
that is a stain. A dirty thing, he says
we have to wash it.

In Patagonia

With a 15 franc copy from the bargain bin
outside Sylvia Beach's famous store, *my God*
was the God of walking. Or so I wanted to believe,

riding toward Leh atop a Kashmiri truck,
through thin untranslated air *as though we, too,*
have journeys mapped out in our central nervous system,

dutifully ordering each day in a cramped
unsteady hand so that my inner life
and journey could finally begin.

But no terra incognita of the mind unfolds
in the monotony of sentences, only indecision,
the failure to climb or break from the country

that could not be trusted or believed,
failure to flee the disappointment stalking
the charmed streets of Hvar that no longer bear

the names I learned to spell out so precisely.
Always thinking toward the dense white heart
of the next trekking season or the year after that,

I was never close *to those desert wanderers,*
who discover in themselves a primeval calmness,
never at the crust of bread and biting.

Remembrance of Things Past

In the parentheses that happen between sleeps.

*

On the blacktop where I preferred not to slam
the tethered yellow ball or join the cadence of play.

*

Alongside a giddy absorption when affection for the narrator
is paramount, floating among pronoun shifts: she and he, you
and I further at sea and much closer than all our fleet imaginings.

*

Stretched out on the couch and rolling
toward the paperbacked thrills of evening,
where the countries we long for occupy a far larger place
in our actual life than the country in which we happen to be.

*

Wanting to pledge allegiance against my parents' orders,
subscribe to the myth of having it both ways,
of reading against the grain for different outcomes
that are not consequences, even as the awful and momentous
transpire in our name on the rocky shale of a desert theatre.

Everybody's Autobiography

The House of Pride
and Other Tales of Hawai'i

In the litany and accounting we could see again.

In the listing and the record we could see and hear,
though none have seen the rail's yellow bill since 1884.

Say there was nothing left but the listing and the recollect
of the nighttime ping, the kioea's warbling query:
how much will you take to leave the Islands and never come back?

Say all of it was intimate and under scrutiny
as we waited in vain for the black mamo's plaintive song
and for the nukupu'u, whose bill was like a small
round hill, whose tale began in a pit-er-iue trill.

For in the listing and the listen everything was personal:
the kamao's swoop and wheel in flight, the police whistles
last heard in the Alaka'i Swamp, the cheep-cheep
of the grosbeak, not seen since 1894
when its clear but quiet halting complaint was halted.

So we listed and believed in the O'ahu ō'ō',
which disappeared so long ago into the litany
and the comfort of the call and repeat,
the dab of unruly blood, the smoke of life and cosmic sap,
and the thin metallic music of the Laysan millerbird,
whose food, the miller moths, continue to abide.

Here is a photograph of the sandstorm that drove
the Laysan honeycreeper to extinction, no distinction
between air and land, wind and sand, no trace
of the up or down-slurred wingbeat, last seen, last heard,
it is said and presumed in the passive voice and emptied
grammatical subject of our century *and in the silence*
from somewhere under the trees, the laugh of a woman, a love-cry.

The House of Mirth

For the womanly and the weary,
for the wound-obsessed,
the sordid details are at hand
and with a basic search we can join
all the other spectators enjoying Lily Bart,

read about the pilfered garbage bag,
the hesitation wounds and prison-
issue blanket, the man who sank
her Oldsmobile and children in the lake,
as God's voice commanded her to action.

In the infamous house, the fixtures
have been changed and the floorboards
seamlessly restained, but the windows
beneath which the impossible took place remain,
bearing witness to the kind of emergency

that lands us side by side in a pool of violence
with the noise of their wings and lives undone,
like atoms whirling away.

Is it the knife that seals it—the postpartum voices
of the unspeakable? Is it the sign some of us
are born to: the moon in retrograde
or Saturn's return? Or the paradoxical effect

of a medicine designed to calm an errant mind
and arrest the spiral descent that from the first
compound sentence reels us in.

Imperator

“You drive like a cowboy,” he says, and when
he repeats, when he calls all accident
a fault and failure, all my dungeon words uncork

and there is no room in the house far back
enough or deep,

no way to scrape away the curse
that has no such daughter
and *dries up the organs of increase.*

*

So young and so untender,
I have battened to his sailor speech,
his “God-damned sons of bitches, cheats

and Cossacks at the door,” but he’s no Lear
turned churlish who *let folly*
in and turned dear judgment out—

He had a bunk in steerage on a ship
of Germans, Poles and fools, a five- or six-
day ocean journey. The ship’s registry records

his dark complexion: a boy with no English
who boarded in Liverpool and limped on broken
hand-sewn boots away from Ellis Island.

*

When I believed myself the chord and song,
the beloved but banished sometime daughter
so young, my lord, and true,

my mirror showed me the detested kite,
that nothing can explain a daughter's villainy
or account for castle fingers, the gouge and tear.

Nothing will come of nothing he says,
though the stage is full and empty and all
the tragic bodies have not yet appeared.

The Godfather

How to separate the shame
from the disarming rush and shock
of recognition when news of several
trashy paragraphs on p. 19 first reached me

and the other sixth graders,
casually smoking against the green
tile and porcelain sinks of the Girls' Room.

Sugared gold in a series of sentences,
a taste for pulp that could be unwrapped,
loosening the lizard mind
into newly bodied motion:

as she glanced over the glass rim,
as she drank, her body bruised,
her lips pulpy.

Easy to return in secret
and always find the astonishment
and surge, there on the bookshelf
(between the Pinter and the Roth)

running my finger over and through,
moving toward *the gasp . . .*
the lightning-like shattering break
and crawling flood . . .

Like the hysteresis effect one sees
with magnetic fields: the lag
between the application and removal
of a force or domain and its subsequent effect
on the simple piece of iron,

which remains magnetized, in thrall,
long after the external field has been removed.

Little House in the Big Woods

O trundle bed and chopping block,
powder and shot, delaine dress
with its strawberry pattern and fabric gloss,

I was never apart and stalwart, never flew
with blankets against a prairie on fire
or with anything but awe in the big woods

of my astonishment—
for Laura and Mary each had a pan
to pour the dark syrup out in little streams.

O semi-circular drive
and window seat, tract dining and living
room kitchens of three-bedroom

half-acre homes, in my own pan
of cubed ice not snow, no sweet
maple leaf hardened toward delight.

Along the strip mall sidewalks
of North Hollywood, no one
tanned my hide, fired Johnny cake

and hardtack to keep the Angel Dusted
otherwise at bay. Laura too
didn't know to mind her manners,

wished she had nothing to wear but skins
and under covers, between pages
of prose, my onlyness startled toward

remove, toward the snug and sparsely
furnished rooms, with Ma and Pa,
good blonde Mary and the hand hewn.

It seems right and horrible
that Mary was left blind, her blue eyes
wiped clear, that many

of God's curses from Exodus descended—
locusts, hail, even death of the first-
born son. Mrs. Wilder

followed the King James and had
a ready psalm or passage for every plight
or trouble: in facing crisis,

Psalm 46. When weary
read Matthew 11, and Romans
8:31–39, and for inward peace,

the 14th chapter of St. John.
Her daughter Rose ghost-wrote
every chapter through every

long winter and much heralded
Minnesota spring and, bachelor girl,
never married.

Everybody's Autobiography

In the filled pages of my sophomore year,
all the writing is all the same with an old
war-movie type of feeling of living

for what had happened and what may happen,
in a past so far removed *I am not I,*
even if my little dog knows me,

but a stranger and vanity and a stream
of bad grammar. Everything revolved
around not having heard and waiting to hear,

waiting for him to finally come out of himself,
adrift in the big velour living-room chair
that did all my talking and the daily news

that didn't mean a thing. Where was Alice?
Where was Anne? Where were Frances
and Sylvia, Dorothy and James?

Where was Helen, and where
was Annie who first spelled w-a-t-e-r
into palms, into hands?

A diary can lead to trouble. For whomsoever
leads any campaign against Islam and Shariah
is ordered to be killed, and Malala,

whose given name means "grief stricken,"
whose pen name is "corn flower," loved
her school uniform, dreaming of artillery fire

in the night, awaking on the bus one day to overhear
"I will kill you," whispered into a cell phone.
It was my father who taught me

to distrust distinctions, lonely in the museum,
unable to express how the paintings made me feel.
Separating the simple subject from the compound

subject particularly, and to begin with the subject I,
wasn't I always all by myself with a new job
in a shoe store and people from another world or time?

Rue de Fleurus

How the story I read last night
haunts and persuades, with its aggrieved

husband wandering around Paris
in the early eighties. His state-of-mind

distraction recalls my own
run-on sentences and ramblings

of distress at the height of my youth
and the throes of a betrayal

I had nearly pushed toward forgetting—
though I can easily recall

the strength of the dollar that year,
the empty tables in Café de Flore

or Brasserie Lipp—and afternoons
spent reading Canetti on a bench

in Square du Vert-Galant.
Below my feet the Seine was moving

and removing the cigarette butt
ashy debris of disappointment

and beneath my gaze the masterpiece
unfolding could not imagine me

but vigorously went to work on Therese,
in long passages that also pummeled my limbs

with the brute exaggerated fists
of the Caretaker. Aghast, enthralled,

unable to board the train away
from there, *the same dark fear*

of knowing and not knowing,
a lozenge on my tongue.

Lovers strolled, the air
was blazing and at the Cinema

Le Champo, "The Battle of Algiers"
was beginning its afternoon run.

On every page of the diary I kept,
between exchange rates,

the cost of wine and cheese,
the weather and names of stations,

a conflagration flares: a litany
of woe, like the one

that fills the postcard of Stein
at home on Rue de Fleurus,

now magically returned
somehow to my hands.

The Beautiful Room Is Empty

Awake again to watch the moon slide back
into the hills, to hear the grackles screech
with the sheer effrontery that thrills a timid
heart, I thought of the way one man I loved
could nod off anywhere, dropping fast,
and how his sleep seeped toward me, a heat
that shushed the insomniac gear and prattle
of night. In the near light before his sleep
strapped me in, *under my gaze, in this creature*
half-natural but half-invented, I conceived
a tenderness in the pause and unleash of his breathing,
desire in the steady pulse at his neck. And I believe
I would have suffered again his indifference
to eat whatever it was that leached from his skin,
to feel it latch on and hold me under until morning.

The House of Bernarda Alba

For three days the winds badger and fume
their deep song of desire—the *duende*
kicking up its legs

until the windowpane unmakes itself
like the proof of low standards,
the evidence of crimes.

In Spain, my guidebook explains, the *Viento Fuerte*
is driven by cold air flowing downhill
and charged like a great tragedy
with a woman's complaint.

It makes me want to do whatever work
I've been avoiding, as though the opposite
of fear is love and love is fear, and truth is truth.

Lorca knew to paint the inner walls of the household yellow
and paint their faces all the same.

He knew a mother's bark and cadence,
the way a mother knows to keep her daughters on a leash,
half-sunk in the bright arena,

like the golden Labrador in Goya's famous painting,
for *a daughter who's disobedient*
becomes an enemy.

In a movie, the Japanese soldier flayed
a Chinese prisoner. In a novel, the Russian colonel
made a Mongol flay a Japanese spy.

What was left would eventually stop screaming
and likewise, the plaster walls and yellow rooms
can dampen any din or racket.

What never takes place nevertheless leaves behind
the carapace of the human, like *the sound of those bells*
that hits you right between the eyes.

And the winds, the devil winds, murder-charged and electric,
sing what cannot be left unsaid in Granada
where Lorca no longer resides or protests.

Look how the dead grass, dried mustard weed
and a few white tail feathers have gathered at the threshold:
omen or offering, cenotaph or curse.

The Eden Express

Twenty-one IDF soldiers were killed
before operations ended and I was barely
twelve kilometers south, studying Hebrew,
living out my labor Zionist indoctrinations
and smoking all the Lebanese hash I could buy.
I was learning fast that *though most diseases*
can be separated from one's self, schizophrenia
is something you are—and leaning toward
their arrogant Sahal training and ancient
Dead Sea salts, the delicate paths of hair
and casual Uzis against half-shut bedroom doors.
Raised on civil disobedience and black-
is-beautiful rallies against apartheid, I still let
the dirty blue Arab buses pass me on the road
to Nahariya. After Fatah on the beach at Haifa
and the red Egged bus of unimaginable fall-
to-pieces flesh, it was hard to recognize myself
on the wrong sides of borders and the uprising
still to come. For seven days in March, I rode
to the citrus fields with armed guards in my wagon
as Katyusha rockets fell and five hundred turkeys
suffocated in their pens. Sleeping in bomb shelters
and sleepless on the guesthouse balcony *more*
and more miserable, shakier and shakier as sweat
spread across the surface of my skin, I watched
and listened to the mechanical *sturm unt drang*
of the night-long stream of tanks driving 25,000
armored souls toward Lake Litani "to root out
the evil weed" and "drive the cockroaches
from their nests." In the weeks that followed
I heard exactly nothing from the Moshes and Darons,
the Tals and Amitais back from reserve duty,
of 285,000 refugees, 6,000 fallen homes, four

strangled Lebanese peasants found in a well.
Which ones danced with me in the volunteers'
lounge and who bruised my American mouth
on the beach at Achziv with all the urgency
of a soldier? A few years later, which ones
blocked the exits at Sabra and Shatila, firing flares
that lit the camp up like a football stadium
as I continued to let hormones crush the odor and burning,
the roll of tanks and unended future of returning.

Civilization and Its Discontents

The voices on the radio have nothing
to do with weeping for those young men
from rural areas in the mid-west and the west,
who have access to firearms and drugstores, who fell
into the high-risk categories and through
the cracks and safety nets, the detailed protocols
of warrior resiliency *as those forces,*
which ordinarily inhibit, ceased to operate.

Anyone who isn't colorblind could see
the red flags: when stateside is a combat
zone of sleeping trouble and shortness of breath,
when the bullet catcher cannot drive
his Ford Escape along the ordinary
Michigan highway unraveling before him
or unmake the jumpiness and rapid heartbeat
or get those boots off fast enough the first time
he saw the light go out in a good man's eyes.

Troubled by headaches. Troubled by memories
and checking off "more than half the time"
on the mental-health questionnaire,
(revealing men as savage beasts to whom
the thought of sparing their own kind is alien)
every soldier at home and over there is fully versed
in suicide prevention training,
in civilization and its discontents.

The one who does all the talking says,
"You don't go ask for help because you'd lose
security clearance, be looked down on and undermine
a whole career," and anyway, by then the super highway
is taking him—the red flags all falling and arriving.

The Jungle Book

All the lexicons and glossaries,
the dictionary glass menageries
can never describe or portray
the comfort bears know

in their comfortable paws
or the mad rush and blaze and hullabaloo
of the wild elephant drive.

Among inland housecat
back yard weeds, kin
to the terrible monkeys

who have no law, no speech,
but the stolen words they overhear
as they wait up above in the branches,

I could not perfect
the wolverine howl, imperial
rhythm and rhyme royal,

though in my humanimal dream
a lion could talk and a book
could stitch me to a future tense,

that almost scent, diffuse
and useless scent of almost belong.

The Golden Notebook

knew how everything would be exposed:
the loveless marriage, off-white lies

and the final gambit of not-speaking.
There was the life (classes, library,

café au lait) *and the man whom I knew*
quite well would never come to me again.

The notebooks lived the other lives
which were more and less and in between—

a bleed and blundering of borders.
My own selves colored there, dark outlines

filling in like news of nuns' bodies
pulled by ropes from shallow graves

in El Salvador. *Instead of a beautiful thing,*
there was a mass of fragments and pieces:

long afternoons reading to find or lose
myself, to burrow toward a time when love

no longer *put my intelligence to sleep*
and with my willing connivance, each page

an abode, as cells turned over
and sister chromosomes migrated

toward opposite poles. But in the nights
spent dreaming of substrate and phosphate,

irreversible reactions still lay hands on me,
ran rough-shod and didn't blink

like an enemy or an old friend one has known
too well and doesn't want to see.

Even when I sunbathed beside Hearst pool,
hanging on every word as a girl I didn't know

described the assault in broad daylight,
with every word, a red or yellow leaf

twisted free, exposing desires as perversions
that made the starlings bank and wheel.

I wanted to put my body upon the gears
and wheels, upon the levers and all the machinery,

for I had seen the places on the girl's head
where hair was missing and touched

the organ of repeat the separated notebooks
could not contain: a white hot running up against

the armored heart of wind. With all nine planets
aligned behind the sun and Prince William

waiting to be born, I resolved to rove,
the cold of loneliness all around me.

The Poetics of Space

The Interpretation of Dreams

after a painting by Mary McDonnell

The cement floor's in camouflage: paint
daubed and Colorado residued
with rain-speckled bird droppings. Un-
diluted cadmium, gunmetal, and cyanine
layer past the edges to create the ghostly
demarcations beside which the painter
squatted down or knelt in splattered jeans,
splattered running shoes to squeegee scrape
flatten and subdue the restless mind
that gropes toward momentum now and in memory
of the red-eyed vireo's wheel and veer
against the firmament; the icy wind and boom
of an icy winter river's underside; first sighting
of forsythia, *the desired unraveling of dream*
or obsessional idea or whatever it may be.

And if you listened carefully, hot trails
of mute exploding bombs were also falling
there or here, and in the nightly otherwhere
on within behind inside the TV screen:
the smart, the scatter and the heat-seeking,
all descending with the gravity
and conviction of the smashingly concrete.

On the Natural History of Destruction

Forty warm minutes in the warming sun. Salt air
masks *the bleak depression that refuses to lift.*

Two secret drops of morphine in his tea
for the everywhere pain he says he'll weather,

for feet swollen and distorted, each toe
a pink scaly balloon of hurts me.

Night is an ocean that always arrives to rattle
and drown. Night is a dangerous confusion

of underwater rustling and climbing moans
where he sleeps at the very edge of disaster,

pillow abandoned to the bed and to the creature
whose webbed wings stretch across the sheets.

Back of the nightstand, the iron sedative
is out of the bag. Purchased in Chicago,

1948, its handle inlaid with mother of pearl,
its Russian-roulette rotating chamber agape.

The zippered pouch is open too—
one bullet rolls free, the ocean in a drawer.

Muscle Memory

Deep in the canyons, low in the canyons
where thunder presses the undersides

of rock, most of the water pillows white
against the granite face but enough

disappears to unmake and take you
from your blue trusty boat, from beside;

against; between; and through to under
and underneath, though you completed

each sentence with the correct preposition,
keeping your eyes on the horizon's eye,

not Calvino's invisible cities of undercuts
and rock sieves, *the melancholy and relief*

of knowing you shall soon give up any thought
of knowing and understanding them.

For the river smacks your hesitate
and didn't see and shows you something

altogether rocky bottom murky green
and if no head down, hip snap, twisting glide

of torso turns you over, you are trapped
and moving in the noisome river silence.

Try not to think thoughts no one should think,
where her thoughts went and when she knew

for certain. Let all the muscles of the spine
memory and remember, not the under

and the underneath, not bronchioles
unbranching in the lungs, alveoli

bursting shut or her blood beating gasps
and sentences into a shuttered brain

where thunder presses and the water
bellows white, low in the canyons

of a city where the buildings have spiral
staircases encrusted with spiral seashells,

in the inside of disappear, the un-
wind of underneath and down there.

A Narrow Road

a partial pecha kucha, after Terrance Hayes

[Miracle of Minamisōma]

In all of these, Freud found, *the uncanny (unhomely)*
of story, nightmare, dream—. The smell of mud.
A mud-drenched shoe poking up from rubble.
A village washed thirty feet southeast
and four feet down into the earth.

[Broken road]

Basho says the sun the moon the days
the months and years are travelers.
The journey itself is home. In Tokyo I had no business
but speech and listening: like a bat in flight
and asleep, I hovered blindly between bird and rat.

[Sendai sunrise]

Full force. Washed out. No vegetables or meat.
The night is thick with dream: another whirlpool
in the harbor, black water like a train moving ninety miles
an hour, and every morning with the tide,
Basho's fish, eyes full of tears—ferry past their doors.

[Earthquake victims]

When Basho walked his narrow road
Louis XIV was in Versailles and Newton
had found gravity. The Oshu-kaido took him
through Sendai and Ishinomaki: the inns where he stayed
are rubble now, twisted cable wires, mud and slime.

[Memories amid rubble]

How to say and write the name of Fujitsuka
or Hanamaki both completely submerged? To speak
Hirota Bay, Hitachinaka, Ishinomaki, where Basho
slept? Say that Iwaki and Iwanuma were flattened
and Kesennuma blazed for days? That Kuji and Otsuchi
were swept into the sea and Minamisanriku is the town
that disappeared? No trace? Erased? Crossed out
like Ofunato and Rikuzentakata. Likewise Omoto,
Orai Town and Ozashi? Ryoishi, Sukagawa, Tanohata
Village, Yamada-machi? All swept, all vanished,
submerged and sunken, all swallowed by the sea.

[Cocooned against the cold]

Like me, the fleets of Gaijin volunteers absorbed
the hard lesson of the cherry trees, their brief pale
blossomings above our heads in Ueno Park. They learned
"hisaichi" for disaster site, to recognize the "mono no aware,"
sadness of things, to stress or not stress every syllable.

[Leaving home]

A wave alters the ecology of the land it rushes up
against and over. And hypothermia slows the tongue
as well, distorting the lake of language in the man
who cannot say "wife swept away" "carried out to sea"
or name the pine of Takekuma Basho never got to see.

[Wrecked cars]

In the famous painted screens from Edo,
waves swirl in gold and silver, churning over and around
the two hundred and sixty-five pine-
covered islands of Matsushima as though
Tawaraya were a sparrow who could fly into the future.

[Power plant ablaze]

From the Edo blaze of 1682, Basho learned
life is a house on fire and set out to walk
and write his northern road and haibun interior.
The earthquake and tsunami are not mine but make
a narrow path I follow north, toward the syllables.

[Tsunami-tossed boat]

Hokusai loved to depict water in motion:
the foam breaking into claws that grasp, the yin
and the yang of empty space under it. Basho borrowed
his name from the banana tree that bears no fruit:
his art and life, pure "ma," pure Prussian blue.

[Disinfecting the damage]

Much has been made of the Japanese spirit,
of the unmoving videotaped faces impassively weeping,
that there is no Japanese word for grief. On TV the fire chief
whose crew rushed to shut the giant harbor gates
sobbed with no "enryo-shasshi," no shame.

[Muddy wasteland]

My students laughed but were dismayed to learn
I ate lunch at the guru-guru sushi place in Shibuya
and shopped for dresses at the supermarket.
One explained the terrible weight of being known always
as "Hibakusha," the atomic-bomb-affected people.

[Survivors' sorrow]

"Gambatte kudasai," people say in passing.
I thought "good luck" or "have a good one"
and said it too—not "please endure it," which is truer
to the stench of rotted fish, the carrion crows
that squawk and caw above abandoned streets.

[Communication barrier]

Built to keep the barbarians to the north, the Shirakawa Barrier
was destroyed even before Basho's time. It was always
an imaginary boundary where culture stopped, like the wall
at Yoshima-hama that could not halt the sea's limitless arrival
as everything meant to remain hidden came into the open.

A Passage to India

> *Revered monks and people. This public rally is aimed at informing the whole world . . . that the entire people entertain the keenest desire for a multiparty democratic system of government.*
>
> —Aung San Suu Kyi

When the Buddha's hairs were carried
to Shwedagon, the great pagoda,

the blind beheld objects, the dumb spoke
and all the deciduous trees of the Himalaya

blossomed out of season with *a radiance*
that belonged neither to water nor moonlight

but stood like a luminous sheaf upon darkness.
Oh blue star of sapphire, oh ruby in the palm,

on the Burmese Road to Socialism
it was shoestring and backpack,

riding old bicycles toward the hundred-fold
horizon line of crumbling pagodas—some close,

some painted yellow, some collapsed
into the far away and fallen kingdom of Pagan.

You ate hot but perhaps too rich, hankered
and sought, wrangled and were no bargain

on the overnight train from Rangoon
to Mandalay, though you tried to read yourself

apart from Miss Quested's rigid paleness,
her growing *tired of seeing picturesque figures pass*

as a frieze. And as you scoured the marketplace
for a perfect set of opium weights, in the palaces

of unreason Director General Win also paid attention
to his dreams, declaring all 100 kyat notes worthless—

wiping out bank accounts *as though the kindest thing*
one can do to a native is to let him die.

As we made our way, a line of monks
in red and rose were circling the great pagoda,

their begging bowls overturned with "no"
and she whose name means Bright Collection

of Strange Victories was already picturing
the pavilion of her speech, the three thousand dead

by mid-September, and the long rainy street
of house arrest. Two weeks later, you watched

on a Bangkok TV as students and monks
and people in white ordinary shirts poured

into the streets, tired of paying for the black
market rice that made your trip cheap.

The Poetics of Space

When among all the other drivers
on the Roosevelt Expressway you brake
to a stop beside where he has fallen
or lain down to sleep it off in the turning lane
and after removing his ratty shirt and filthy
Levi's—it happens that quickly—*defeated*
by the resonances he keeps trying to describe,
he reaches through the driver's-side window
to scratch your face and pull you by the hair
toward the ones who all this time he
has been talking and talking to, who wouldn't

try to make it stop, and frantic, raise
the automatic window, catching him
beneath the arm until his cry of pain
and terror matches yours exactly, and like
the indifferent drivers all around you, step
with real fear hard on the accelerator
to gun it toward away from there,
the consolations of good listeners?

For isn't their sympathy and outrage
well deserved for best intentions, your
tried for Christ's sake bloodied face to help
and what else could anyone, would anyone
do, when faced directly with *the act itself*
the sudden flare up of being suddenly
unconstrained or confined to the imagination?

Tales of the Grotesque and Arabesque

Fresh back from Iraq and battle-tested,
their M-16s locked and loaded,
three hundred National Guardsmen landed
where the law and order situation was bad

and before they let the people flood
the Mardi-Gras-colored seats,
they cordoned off the astroturf
and searched and seized the cigarettes and pen knives,

lighters and bottles from those who could have stayed
and watched the roof blow, their TV sets
and couches swamped and swallowed.

In the Superdome they were suspect and safe,
though in the air above the stadium where pigeons fly,
there was a desperate SOS, *the low stifled sound*
that arises from the soul when overcharged with awe,

when there is no quarterbacked command, no coach,
no concerted drive into the end zone.

*

For we think when natural disaster comes
it comes for everyone, and we will stop our cars
or rise from benches to help, but inside
that August's Superdome no game-saving Hail Mary

came just in time and only rumor floated:
rumors of individuals robbed and beaten,
individuals raped in the third tier bathroom stalls

or was it at the five or fifty yard line?
Individuals who had to pee on the floor,
who spoke of the pervading stench,

of no electricity and the shouts for order,
as Kayresa Newman's baby passed out in her arms.

And then my soul sickened and became giddy
with the giddiness of one who gazes downward
into some dreary and unfathomable abyss.

*

It was scary. We have bodies. We have strokes
and chest pain, seizures and fainting. There were bodies
so tightly packed the guardsmen couldn't pass between
the hungry little voices grabbing in to pull and scratch,

the echo of gunshots unmasking them as refugees,
so like ourselves and more ourselves than we had ever been,
as twenty thousand swamped the hundred-fifty-
dollar boxes and hundred-dollar seats.

Who or what became them in the dark aisles
of that dank arena but the human dark of blank refusal
and blackout calm before the emergency kicked in,
before the storm peeled the cover off
the stadium roof and two large holes let rain and light

fall on the elderly woman dead in a wheelchair
with a note on her lap bearing our names.

*

Were they being treated like animals by animals,
behaving like animals, or rising and falling
to a natural level of self-annihilation

as outside the Superdome, the 82nd Airborne
was having trouble distinguishing between degrees
of need, between disaster and disgrace *with the low, dull sound*
a watch makes when enveloped in cotton.

If his house is ruined there is nothing he can do
and nobody in charge to hold accountable
as yellow school buses caught in traffic jams
and able bodies pressed into panic against the barricades.

In the rising heat that was scramble and riot,
no spontaneous human wave of triumph could raise
our arms, one after the other, or move us to stand.

For My Father Who Was Nothing like Atticus Finch

Nothing helped that day before the day:
not walking, or sitting, not lying at an incline.
We shuffled through all the rooms of business,
used the tray and straw for the fresh-squeezed juice.

"Take it away," he hissed, one of the last
he managed before the wheezy whistle gurgle
(a sure sign, the nurses said) entered the room
with the afternoon sun and lit up all the dust

and pockets of resistance, insisting *mockingbirds*
don't do one thing but sing their hearts out for us.

I put my face against his then and whispered too,
helped him climb back onto the hospital bed
where he lay down his bird bones and startled up
the rattle breath, in earnest.

Iron Century

Full with schadenfreude
for my own everyday losses,
my shimmering mess of pottage,

I have no last, no testament,
nor children, nor poor relations
to bestow my kernel of inheritance:

the house and harbor lights, a few
leather-bound volumes, the purple toes
and fish-out-of-water breathing.

In a cold war, in my father's century,
when all that remained of Clementis
was the cap on Gottwald's head

in a book of laughter and forgetting,
he was cold as ice and circling—
like Pluto, frozen god-king

of the frozen underworld,
now casually downgraded
at a meeting of astronomers

to dwarf or fairly large rock (FLR)—
without enough gravity to dominate
the neighborhood of his orbit.

And in the classroom model
of our solar system, in the space
where the ninth wire holder once bore

its white unbreakable ball: a caesura
a world where the fearsome laughter
of the angels drowns all our words

with its jangle. When my father pulled
from his orbit, exhibiting all the signs
I was green enough and salad,

cold in blood enough to pull
my hand away from that final
painful grip and wave.

Shirt Stained Ochre

When I returned like *the traveler*
belonging no more to one place
than to the next, and finally arrived

at the station that marked the end
and beginning of where one of us
was from, the border guard intoned:

"one citizen, one alien," pulling us aside
to unfold our moneybelts and open
our trunk, unwinding the prayer wheels'

scrolls of secret writing to display
the secret code within.
"Ohm Mane Padme Ohm?" I intoned

in response to his question. Under a light
as white as the unsheltered sky
in Fez or Marrakesh, his dogs sniffed

among the ten thousand small paper packages
and unset semi-precious stones
I had carried home from Rajasthan,

translating us back
to the country of my birth.

Letters to a Young Poet

Out of our arguments with ourselves, what is lost
in translation is news that stays news, a small (or large)
machine made of words that makes nothing
happen, comes nearer to vital truth than history,
and must go in fear, be as new as foam, as old
as the rock, have something in it that is barbaric,
vast and wild, a way of taking life by the throat.
And out of this turning within, out of this immersion
in your own world, as if the top of my head were taken off
for lack of what is found there or in the journal
of a sea animal living on land, wanting to fly in the sky,
in the best words, in the best order, put things before
his eyes: imaginary gardens with real toads that spring
from genuine feeling that the mind is dangerous
and my whole body so cold no fire can ever warm me—

NOTES

Italicized lines are borrowed from the books referred to in the titles or mentioned in the bodies of the poems.

"Beyond the Pleasure Principle": The names: Hayder Sabber Abd, Shalan Said Al Sharoni, Miktub Al-Boodi, Thaar Salman Dawood, Abdou Hussain Sa'ad Faleh, Asad Hamza Hanfosh, Kasim Mehaddi Hilas, Amjad Iraqi, Manadel al-Jamadi, Mohanded Juma Juma, Mustafa Jassim Mustafa, Nori Samir Gunbar Al-Yasseri, Ameen Sa'eed Al-Sheikh, Hussein Mohussein Mata Al-Zayiadi, Abd Alwhab Youss.

"The Anatomy of Melancholy": Information and phrases are adapted from articles in the *New York Times*, the website of the NIMH Mood and Anxiety Disorders Program 2004, and Aaron T. Beck's *Depression: Causes and Treatment* (University of Pennsylvania Press 1967).

"The House of Pride and Other Tales of Hawai'i": Information about extinct bird species of Hawai'i was found at www.birdinghawaii.co.uk.

"Imperator": SS Imperator is the name of an ocean liner built for the *Hamburg America Line* and launched in 1912. It is the ship my father sailed on when he emigrated from Poland to the US.

"Everybody's Autobiography": In 2009 Malala Yousafzai, a school girl from the Swat Valley in Pakistan, kept a diary that was published by the BBC. Her observations were published under the pseudonym Gul Makai. In 2014 Malala Yousafzai was awarded the Nobel Peace Prize.

"The Eden Express": Historical information and quotations are adapted and borrowed from Robert Fisk's *Pity the Nation: The Abduction of Lebanon* (Nation Books 2002).

"Muscle Memory": For Dale Herrick.

"A Narrow Road": Basho's *The Narrow Road to Oku* is a standard text read by Japanese school children. It is a travelogue as well as poetry, recording Basho's final "walking tour." Part of that final journey went through the Kansai area of Japan. A *pecha kucha* is a Japanese presentation format that Terrance Hayes turned into a poetic form. This poem responds to a series of photographs on the National Geographic website, "Twenty Unforgettable Photographs."

"A Passage to India": The epigraph is from Aung San Suk Kyi's speech on August 26, 1988 during the 8888 Pro-Democracy Movement in Burma.

"Tales of the Grotesque and Arabesque": Information and phrases in the poem are adapted from articles that originally appeared in *The Times Picayune* during September of 2005 and from *Voices from the Storm: The People of New Orleans on Hurricane Katrina and Its Aftermath* (McSweeney's 2006).

ABOUT THE AUTHOR

Lisa Sewell is the author of *The Way Out* (Alice James Books 1998), *Name Withheld* (Four Way Books 2006), and *Long Corridor* (Seven Kitches Press 2009), which received the 2008 Keystone Chapbook award. She is also co-editor, with Claudia Rankine, of *American Poets in the 21st Century: The New Poetics* (Wesleyan 2007) and *Eleven More American Women Poets in the 21st Century: Poetics Across North America* (Wesleyan 2012). She has received grants and awards from the Leeway Foundation, the National Endowment for the Arts, the Pennsylvania Council on the Arts, and the Fine Arts Work Center at Provincetown, and has held residencies at the Virginia Center for the Creative Arts, the MacDowell Colony, Yaddo, Fundacion Valparaiso, and the Tyrone Guthrie Center. She lives in Philadelphia and teaches at Villanova University.

ABOUT THE ARTIST

Endi Poskovic is a print artist whose graphic imagery suggests dichotomies that exist in life and whose visual narratives explore universal themes of displacement, memory, transformation, and revival. Educated in Yugoslavia, Norway, and the United States, Poskovic has exhibited in numerous international forums and has been the recipient of fellowships and grants from the Guggenheim Foundation, Rockefeller-Bellagio, Pollock-Krasner, Camargo, Flemish Ministry of Culture, Norwegian Government, New York State Council on the Arts, Art Matters, and many others. Poskovic's work is in public collections worldwide, including Harvard University Fogg Art Museum, Detroit Institute of the Arts, Royal Antwerp Museum of Fine Arts, and Philadelphia Museum of Art. He is a Professor at the University of Michigan where he teaches in the Stamps School of Art and Design, and Center for Russian, East European, and Eurasian Studies.

ABOUT THE WORD WORKS

The Word Works, a nonprofit literary organization, publishes contemporary poetry and presents public programs. Our imprints include The Washington Prize, International Editions, the Hilary Tham Capital Collection, and The Tenth Gate Prize. A reading period is also held in May.

Monthly, The Word Works offers free literary programs in the Chevy Chase, MD, Café Muse series, and each summer, it holds free poetry programs in Washington, D.C.'s Rock Creek Park. Annually in June, two high school students debut in the Joaquin Miller Poetry Series as winners of the Jacklyn Potter Young Poets Competition. Since 1974, Word Works programs have included: "In the Shadow of the Capitol," a symposium and archival project on the African American intellectual community in segregated Washington, D.C.; the Gunston Arts Center Poetry Series; the Poet Editor panel discussions at The Writer's Center; and Master Class workshops.

As a 501(c)3 organization, The Word Works has received awards from the National Endowment for the Arts, the National Endowment for the Humanities, the D.C. Commission on the Arts & Humanities, the Witter Bynner Foundation, Poets & Writers, The Writer's Center, Bell Atlantic, the David G. Taft Foundation, and others, including many generous private patrons.

The Word Works has established an archive of artistic and administrative materials in the Washington Writing Archive housed in the George Washington University Gelman Library. It is a member of the Council of Literary Magazines and Presses and its books are distributed by Small Press Distribution.

More information at WordWorksBooks.org.

ABOUT THE TENTH GATE PRIZE

Founded by Series Editor Leslie McGrath, the prize honors the work and poetics of Jane Hirshfield and promotes the work of mid-career poets. Americans and Canadians poets with two or more published collections may submit between June 1 and July 15.

THANK YOU to the generous contributors who helped to launch this imprint: Patricia Absher, Karren Alenier, Nathalie F. Anderson, James Beall, Cliff Bernier, Jean Bower, Christopher Bursk, Lynn and Jeff Callahan, Nancy Naomi Carlson, Grace Cavalieri, Maria Coughlin, Payton Cuddy, Mark Cugini, George Drew, Christopher J. Dujardin, W. Perry Epes, Teri Foltz, Hans Gallas, Barbara Goldberg, Sarah Gorham-Skinner, Paul Grayson, Clarinda Harriss, Michael Hauptschein, Jens T. Hinrichs, Hudson Valley Writers Center, Stephen Hubbard, Leigh Jackson, Myong-Hee Kim, Fred Marchant, Marilyn McCabe, Kathleen McCoy, Ann McLaughlin, Laura Orem, Dwaine Rieves, Enid Shomer, Margo Taft Stever, Yancey Strickler, Adam Tavel, William Taylor, Barbara Ungar, Stuart Vyse, Charlotte Warren, Nancy White, Diane Williams, Anne C. Wind, Anne Harding Woodworth, and Katherine E. Young.

OTHER WORD WORKS BOOKS

INTERNATIONAL EDITIONS

Keyne Cheshire (trans.), *Murder at Jagged Rock: A Tragedy by Sophocles*
Yoko Danno & James C. Hopkins, *The Blue Door*
Moshe Dor, Barbara Goldberg, Giora Leshem, eds., *The Stones Remember: Native Israeli Poets*
Moshe Dor (Barbara Goldberg, trans.), *Scorched by the Sun*
Lee Sang (Myong-Hee Kim, trans.), *Crow's Eye View: The Infamy of Lee Sang, Korean Poet*
Vladimir Levchev (Henry Taylor, trans.), *Black Book of the Endangered Species*

THE HILARY THAM CAPITAL COLLECTION

Mel Belin, *Flesh That Was Chrysalis*
Doris Brody, *Judging the Distance*
Sarah Browning, *Whiskey in the Garden of Eden*
Grace Cavalieri, *Pinecrest Rest Home*
Christopher Conlon, *Gilbert and Garbo in Love*
& *Mary Falls: Requiem for Mrs. Surratt*
Donna Denizé, *Broken like Job*
W. Perry Epes, *Nothing Happened*
Bernadette Geyer, *The Scabbard of Her Throat*
Barbara G. S. Hagerty, *Twinzilla*
James Hopkins, *Eight Pale Women*
Brandon Johnson, *Love's Skin*
Marilyn McCabe, *Perpetual Motion*
Judith McCombs, *The Habit of Fire*
James McEwen, *Snake Country*
Miles David Moore, *The Bears of Paris*
& *Rollercoaster*
Kathi Morrison-Taylor, *By the Nest*
Michael Shaffner, *The Good Opinion of Squirrels*
Maria Terrone, *The Bodies We Were Loaned*
Hilary Tham, *Bad Names for Women*
& *Counting*
Barbara Louise Ungar, *Charlotte Brontë, You Ruined My Life*
& *Immortal Medusa*
Jonathan Vaile, *Blue Cowboy*
Tera Vale Ragan, *Reading the Ground*
Rosemary Winslow, *Green Bodies*
Michele Wolf, *Immersion*
Joseph Zealberg, *Covalence*

THE WASHINGTON PRIZE

Nathalie F. Anderson, *Following Fred Astaire*, 1998
Michael Atkinson, *One Hundred Children Waiting for a Train*, 2001
Molly Bashaw, *The Whole Field Still Moving Inside It*, 2013
Carrie Bennett, *biography of water*, 2004
Peter Blair, *Last Heat*, 1999
John Bradley, *Love-in-Idleness: The Poetry of Roberto Zingarello*, 1995, 2nd edition 2015
Richard Carr, *Ace*, 2008
Jamison Crabtree, *Rel[AM]ent*, 2014
B. K. Fischer, *St. Rage's Vault*, 2012
Ann Rae Jonas, *A Diamond Is Hard But Not Tough*, 1997
Frannie Lindsay, *Mayweed*, 2009
Richard Lyons, *Fleur Carnivore*, 2005
Fred Marchant, *Tipping Point*, 1993, 2nd edition 2013
Ron Mohring, *Survivable World*, 2003
Barbara Moore, *Farewell to the Body*, 1990
Brad Richard, *Motion Studies*, 2010
Jay Rogoff, *The Cutoff*, 1994
Prartho Sereno, *Call from Paris*, 2007, 2nd edition 2013
Enid Shomer, *Stalking the Florida Panther*, 1987
John Surowiecki, *The Hat City After Men Stopped Wearing Hats*, 2006
Miles Waggener, *Phoenix Suites*, 2002
Mike White, *How to Make a Bird with Two Hands*, 2011
Nancy White, *Sun, Moon, Salt*, 1992, 2nd edition 2010

ADDITIONAL TITLES

Karren L. Alenier, *Wandering on the Outside*
Karren L. Alenier, Hilary Tham, Miles David Moore, eds., *Winners: A Retrospective of the Washington Prize*
Christopher Bursk, ed., *Cool Fire*
Barbara Goldberg, *Berta Broadfoot and Pepin the Short*
W.T. Pfefferle, *My Coolest Shirt*
Jacklyn Potter, Dwaine Rieves, Gary Stein, eds., *Cabin Fever: Poets at Joaquin Miller's Cabin*
Robert Sargent, *Aspects of a Southern Story* & *A Woman From Memphis*

CPSIA information can be obtained at www.ICGtesting.com
Printed in the USA
BVOW05s1043170315

392042BV00001B/2/P

9 780915 380961